Gardening PLANNER

Gardening Planner

ISBN: 978-1987585193

Created by Just Plan Books

About This Book

This garden planner has been created to make gardening a breeze. Keeping on top of what jobs need doing (and when) can be a particular challenge when growing fruits and vegetables.

The basics of when to sow, plant out, and harvest can be complex enough between different varieties of carrot. Add in concerns over which bugs might eat the sprouts this month, when to water, feed, or protect from the elements and it can fast become a complex operation.

PLANTS AND GARDEN

Plant Inventory - No more hunting for seed packets; record that information here. Note down the space required, location, and any pests or diseases to be on the lookout for. Record recommended or actual sowing dates and estimate when to plant out and harvest.

Garden Design - Plan out your plot on squared pages to make sure spacing and location are correct for each plant.

PLANNING

Year Planner - An at a glance overview of the entire year. Plan and organise tasks by both season and month.

Recurring Tasks - Watering, feeding, mowing - list recurring tasks here as a quick reference guide and organise them into daily, weekly, monthly, and yearly tasks.

Undated Month Planner - Plan and organise tasks for the month with a four weekly planning page. List which plants to sow, plant out, and harvest, along with jobs to do, pests to watch out for, purchases to make, and notes.

NOTES AND LISTS

Spending Tracker - Track any purchases along with a running total and stay in control of costs.

Lists - Handy checklist pages with space above to categorise as required.

Notes - Plenty of lined pages to make quick notes or add in any insights and tips for future years.

We have designed this book to suit as many gardeners as possible. Whether you are an experienced gardener or just starting out, we hope this book will become an indispensable reference to revisit year after year.

Plants and Garden

PLANT INVENTORY

PLANTS AND GARDEN

PLANT	SOW	PLANT OUT	HARVEST

SPACE REQUIRED	LOCATION	PESTS/DISEASES	NOTES

PLANT INVENTORY

PLANT	SOW	PLANT OUT	HARVEST

SPACE REQUIRED	LOCATION	PESTS/DISEASES	NOTES	
				PLANTS AND GARDEN

PLANT INVENTORY

PLANT	SOW	PLANT OUT	HARVEST

SPACE REQUIRED	LOCATION	PESTS/DISEASES	NOTES

PLANTS AND GARDEN

PLANT INVENTORY

PLANT	SOW	PLANT OUT	HARVEST

SPACE REQUIRED	LOCATION	PESTS/DISEASES	NOTES

PLANT INVENTORY

PLANT	SOW	PLANT OUT	HARVEST

SPACE REQUIRED	LOCATION	PESTS/DISEASES	NOTES

PLANTS AND GARDEN

PLANTS AND GARDEN

PLANT	SOW	PLANT OUT	HARVEST

SPACE REQUIRED	LOCATION	PESTS/DISEASES	NOTES

PLANT INVENTORY

PLANT	SOW	PLANT OUT	HARVEST

SPACE REQUIRED	LOCATION	PESTS/DISEASES	NOTES

PLANT INVENTORY

PLANT	SOW	PLANT OUT	HARVEST

SPACE REQUIRED	LOCATION	PESTS/DISEASES	NOTES

PLANTS AND GARDEN

PLANT INVENTORY

PLANT	SOW	PLANT OUT	HARVEST

SPACE REQUIRED	LOCATION	PESTS/DISEASES	NOTES

PLANTS AND GARDEN

PLANT INVENTORY

PLANT	SOW	PLANT OUT	HARVEST

CATEGORY:

SPACE REQUIRED	LOCATION	PESTS/DISEASES	NOTES

PLANT INVENTORY

PLANT	SOW	PLANT OUT	HARVEST

SPACE REQUIRED	LOCATION	PESTS/DISEASES	NOTES

PLANTS AND GARDEN

PLANT INVENTORY

PLANTS AND GARDEN

PLANT	SOW	PLANT OUT	HARVEST

SPACE REQUIRED	LOCATION	PESTS/DISEASES	NOTES

PLANTS AND GARDEN

PLANT	SOW	PLANT OUT	HARVEST

SPACE REQUIRED	LOCATION	PESTS/DISEASES	NOTES

PLANTS AND GARDEN

PLANT INVENTORY

PLANTS AND GARDEN

PLANT	SOW	PLANT OUT	HARVEST

SPACE REQUIRED	LOCATION	PESTS/DISEASES	NOTES	
				PLANTS AND GARDEN

PLANTS AND GARDEN

PLANT	SOW	PLANT OUT	HARVEST

SPACE REQUIRED	LOCATION	PESTS/DISEASES	NOTES

PLANTS AND GARDEN

SOIL TYPE:

PH LEVEL:

PLANTS AND GARDEN

PLANTS AND GARDEN

Planning

YEAR PLANNER

PLANNING

SPRING

SUMMER

AUTUMN

WINTER

JANUARY	FEBRUARY	MARCH

APRIL	MAY	JUNE

JULY	AUGUST	SEPTEMBER

OCTOBER	NOVEMBER	DECEMBER

PLANNING

YEAR PLANNER

SPRING

SUMMER

AUTUMN

WINTER

JANUARY	FEBRUARY	MARCH

APRIL	MAY	JUNE

JULY	AUGUST	SEPTEMBER

OCTOBER	NOVEMBER	DECEMBER

PLANNING

PLANNING

DAILY

WEEKLY

MONTHLY

YEARLY

DAILY

WEEKLY

MONTHLY

YEARLY

MONTHLY PLANNER

SOW	PLANT OUT	HARVEST	JOBS

PESTS/DISEASES	PURCHASES	NOTES

MONTH:

WEEK 1

WEEK 2

WEEK 3

WEEK 4

PLANNING

MONTHLY PLANNER

SOW	PLANT OUT	HARVEST	JOBS

PESTS/DISEASES	PURCHASES	NOTES

MONTH:

WEEK 1

WEEK 2

WEEK 3

WEEK 4

PLANNING

SOW	PLANT OUT	HARVEST	JOBS

PLANNING

PESTS/DISEASES	PURCHASES	NOTES

MONTH:

WEEK 1	WEEK 2

WEEK 3	WEEK 4

PLANNING

MONTHLY
PLANNER

PLANNING

SOW	PLANT OUT	HARVEST	JOBS

PESTS/DISEASES	PURCHASES	NOTES

MONTH:

WEEK 1

WEEK 2

WEEK 3

WEEK 4

MONTHLY PLANNER

PLANNING

SOW	PLANT OUT	HARVEST	JOBS

PESTS/DISEASES	PURCHASES	NOTES

WEEK 1

WEEK 2

WEEK 3

WEEK 4

PLANNING

MONTHLY PLANNER

PLANNING

SOW	PLANT OUT	HARVEST	JOBS

PESTS/DISEASES	PURCHASES	NOTES

WEEK 1	WEEK 2

WEEK 3	WEEK 4

PLANNING

MONTHLY PLANNER

SOW	PLANT OUT	HARVEST	JOBS

PESTS/DISEASES	PURCHASES	NOTES

MONTH:

WEEK 1	WEEK 2

WEEK 3	WEEK 4

PLANNING

MONTHLY PLANNER

SOW	PLANT OUT	HARVEST	JOBS

PESTS/DISEASES	PURCHASES	NOTES

WEEK 1	WEEK 2

WEEK 3	WEEK 4

PLANNING

MONTHLY PLANNER

PLANNING

SOW	PLANT OUT	HARVEST	JOBS

PESTS/DISEASES	PURCHASES	NOTES

MONTH:

WEEK 1	WEEK 2

WEEK 3	WEEK 4

PLANNING

MONTHLY PLANNER

SOW	PLANT OUT	HARVEST	JOBS

PESTS/DISEASES	PURCHASES	NOTES

MONTH:

WEEK 1

WEEK 2

WEEK 3

WEEK 4

PLANNING

PLANNING

SOW	PLANT OUT	HARVEST	JOBS

PESTS/DISEASES	PURCHASES	NOTES

WEEK 1	WEEK 2

WEEK 3	WEEK 4

PLANNING

MONTHLY PLANNER

PLANNING

SOW	PLANT OUT	HARVEST	JOBS

PESTS/DISEASES	PURCHASES	NOTES

MONTH:

WEEK 1	WEEK 2

WEEK 3	WEEK 4

PLANNING

SOW	PLANT OUT	HARVEST	JOBS

PLANNING

PESTS/DISEASES	PURCHASES	NOTES

MONTH:

WEEK 1	WEEK 2

WEEK 3	WEEK 4

PLANNING

MONTHLY PLANNER

SOW	PLANT OUT	HARVEST	JOBS

PESTS/DISEASES	PURCHASES	NOTES

PLANNING

WEEK 1

WEEK 2

WEEK 3

WEEK 4

PLANNING

MONTHLY PLANNER

PLANNING

SOW	PLANT OUT	HARVEST	JOBS

PESTS/DISEASES	PURCHASES	NOTES

WEEK 1

WEEK 2

WEEK 3

WEEK 4

PLANNING

MONTHLY PLANNER

SOW	PLANT OUT	HARVEST	JOBS

PESTS/DISEASES	PURCHASES	NOTES

WEEK 1

WEEK 2

WEEK 3

WEEK 4

PLANNING

MONTHLY PLANNER

SOW	PLANT OUT	HARVEST	JOBS

PESTS/DISEASES	PURCHASES	NOTES

MONTH:

WEEK 1	WEEK 2

WEEK 3	WEEK 4

MONTHLY PLANNER

SOW	PLANT OUT	HARVEST	JOBS

PESTS/DISEASES	PURCHASES	NOTES

WEEK 1

WEEK 2

WEEK 3

WEEK 4

PLANNING

MONTHLY PLANNER

SOW	PLANT OUT	HARVEST	JOBS

PESTS/DISEASES	PURCHASES	NOTES

WEEK 1

WEEK 2

WEEK 3

WEEK 4

PLANNING

MONTHLY PLANNER

PLANNING

SOW	PLANT OUT	HARVEST	JOBS

PESTS/DISEASES	PURCHASES	NOTES

MONTH:

WEEK 1	WEEK 2

WEEK 3	WEEK 4

PLANNING

MONTHLY PLANNER

SOW	PLANT OUT	HARVEST	JOBS

PESTS/DISEASES	PURCHASES	NOTES

WEEK 1

WEEK 2

WEEK 3

WEEK 4

PLANNING

MONTHLY PLANNER

PLANNING

SOW	PLANT OUT	HARVEST	JOBS

PESTS/DISEASES	PURCHASES	NOTES

WEEK 1

WEEK 2

WEEK 3

WEEK 4

MONTHLY PLANNER

PLANNING

SOW	PLANT OUT	HARVEST	JOBS

PESTS/DISEASES	PURCHASES	NOTES

WEEK 1

WEEK 2

WEEK 3

WEEK 4

PLANNING

MONTHLY PLANNER

SOW	PLANT OUT	HARVEST	JOBS

PESTS/DISEASES	PURCHASES	NOTES

WEEK 1

WEEK 2

WEEK 3

WEEK 4

PLANNING

Notes and Lists

SPENDING TRACKER

DETAILS	COST	RUNNING TOTAL	DETAILS	COST	RUNNING TOTAL

DETAILS	COST	RUNNING TOTAL	DETAILS	COST	RUNNING TOTAL

NOTES AND LISTS

SPENDING TRACKER

DETAILS	COST	RUNNING TOTAL	DETAILS	COST	RUNNING TOTAL

NOTES AND LISTS

DETAILS	COST	RUNNING TOTAL	DETAILS	COST	RUNNING TOTAL

NOTES AND LISTS

Printed in Great Britain
by Amazon